No Fun in the Woods

Written by
Stephen Rickard

I am in the woods.

I can hear a quack.
I can hear a quack, quack.

It is a duck. A duck is quacking.

Now he can hear the quacking duck.

Will he shoot the quacking duck?

Shut up, duck! Shut up, now!

Hush!

I can hear a buzz.
I can hear a buzz, buzz.

It is a bee. A bee is buzzing.
I can hear a buzzing bee.

Now all the bees are buzzing.
Quick! Run!

Now I can hear a yap.

I can hear a yap, yap, yap.
It is a dog.

'Yap! Yap!' yaps the dog.

The dog wags its tail.

Now it has mud on its legs and on me.

It is such a dim dog.

Can I hear a chug?
Can I hear a chug, chug?

No, I cannot hear a chug, chug.
Are you mad?

I can see a goat,
but a goat cannot chug.

A goat cannot chug, but it can get my hat.

Bad goat!

Can I hear a quack? No.
Can I hear a buzz? No.
Can I hear a yap? No.

It is a bug. I can see a bug.

A bug cannot quack or buzz or yap.

Now I see a mass of bugs.

This is bad. Quick! Run!

Is it fun in the woods?

If that is fun, I am a turnip. You can keep it.

No! I will curl up in my room with my laptop.

Now **this** is fun!